Contents

5. Introduction
7. Baubles Bangles And Poetry
9. A Day At Lowestoft Beach
10. A Doctor's Appointment
12. A Nudist Beach At Southwold?
14. Afternoon Tea
16. All Work And Not Much Play
18. Barbara And The Bin Ben
19. Being Left Handed
22. Blanche's Trip To Bluewater
24. Cecil Lost One Wife Then Got A Life
26. Dame Vera Lynn
28. Dante's Veggie Diet
29. Doreen's Mobility Scooter
31. Elf And Safety In The Fire Service
33. Elsie
35. Henry's Dating Game
37. Ladies In Makeup
39. Little Archie's Card
41. M & S Penny Bazaar
43. My Friend's Trip To Felixstowe
45. My Lost Mail
46. Now I've Got Me Bus Pass
47. On The Cutting Room Floor
50. Our Dog Jason
53. People's Pets
54. Syd-E-Ney The Head Waiter
56. The Antiques Road Show
57. The Apple Gatherers
59. The Cowboy Plumber
61. The Credit Crunch
63. The Deliverymen
65. The Good Old Days
67. The Heat Wave
69. The Ice Cream Jingles
71. The New Shed
73. The Police Flower Show
75. The Sales
77. The Swinging Sixties
79. The Trainee Hairdresser
82. The Vanishing Rooster
84. Time To Do The Garden
85. Welcome Prime Minister
86 When Dolly Gate Crashed
88. When Olga Became A Thespian
90. While Barbara's Away

Acknowledgements

*   *   *

*My sincere thanks must go to Bob Shelley
who has always believed in me.*

*   *   *

*Many thanks to Jasmine Simmons who created the very
humorous illustrations, a student at Kesgrave High School.*

*   *   *

To Don my husband, for his patience.

*   *   *

*Stephen Foster for allowing me airtime, on
his Happy Hour show, on BBC Radio Suffolk.*

*   *   *

*My dear friend Terry Meades who has
helped me tirelessly.*

*   *   *

*Glenn and Annie at Leiston Press printers
must have a huge thank you for printing my
first book for this most deserving charity
"The Tree House Appeal" for children's hospices.*

INTRODUCTION

I was born in Ely. I now live in Oulton Broad with
my husband, where we have lived in the same house
for the last thirty or so years. Where does the time
go? For several years I was a member of the Choral
Society and later joined an amateur dramatic society.
I have always had a way with words, as far back as
my school days. I used to make up rhymes about the
teachers, but all in the best possible taste.

About two years ago I started to do poems on local radio
with Foz and Bob and I have been doing them ever
since.

Jane Mower The Sunrise Poet

Baubles Bangles And Poetry

I collect necklaces by the dozen, I pick them up at
vintage sales.
They're in all shades and sizes they hang on my clothes
rails.
One is red and shiny, really long with great big beads,
I have them in all sizes to cater for my needs.
I had a lovely black one with beads quite large and fine,
but I'm afraid they had a mishap when I went out to
dine.

❊   ❊   ❊

I went off to the ladies and caught them on the door,
the big black beads went everywhere and shot across
the floor.
They looked like big black cockroaches, I tried to find a
broom, I knew I never had much time someone would
come in soon.
This lady looked quite horrified when she saw them
scattered there, she called out for the manageress who
quickly did appear.

❊   ❊   ❊

She said, *"Oh I'll have to ring up Rentokil, health and
safety will be on my case"* I felt quite embarrassed
I didn't know where to put my face.
I explained that it was my necklace that once adorned
my neck, she said *"I'll help you sweep them up"* what
could I say "oh heck!"

I also had a vintage brooch, like Poirot wears on his lapel, I wore it on my sweater it did look rather swell. But when I came to wash it and switched on the machine, my sweater was going round and round, the brooch nowhere to be seen.

❈   ❈   ❈

I found it in three pieces I was really vexed, why am I so forgetful whatever will I do next?
I gathered up the pieces took them to Yarmouth down Market Row, they stuck it back together so no one would ever know.

A Day At Lowestoft Beach

Many years ago in nineteen forty-three me auntie and
me uncle, had a day out by the sea. She'd knitted him a
pair of swimming trunks, in a fetching shade of red.
"My word you look the part" me auntie Violet said.

❊   ❊   ❊

They went in for a paddle, the sea was really cold.
Auntie said, *"Now come on Fred, you really must be bold."*

❊   ❊   ❊

They gingerly waded deeper, the sea up to their neck.
When auntie heard a woman cry,
"Oh look at him! Oh heck!"

❊   ❊   ❊

Fred came slowly back to shore, the wool had all
expanded. The trunks were now down to his feet, and
so he stood there stranded.

❊   ❊   ❊

*"Why did you knit these flipping things? I'm showing all I've
got."* Some woman said, *"I shouldn't worry, you haven't got
a lot."*

❊   ❊   ❊

Poor Fred was so embarrassed as he went back to his
chair. *"If I go on the beach again, I won't be coming
here."*

A Doctor's Appointment

When you've got arthritis, and each day you ache like hell. You think, I'll go to the doctors, I don't feel very well.

❈   ❈   ❈

You sit there in the waiting room, it's full as it can be. You think, when is it my turn, when will they call me.

❈   ❈   ❈

After fifty minutes, the girl calls out your name. The doctor says, *"Just take a seat, you look like you're in pain."*

❈   ❈   ❈

You tell him all your symptoms, while he just clicks on line. He hardly even looks at you, he hasn't got the time.

❈   ❈   ❈

Now you just take these tablets, I think they'll ease the pain. And if they don't, don't worry, just come back again.

❈   ❈   ❈

If you're still here in six months time, and still not feeling better. I'll send you to the hospital, and write you out a letter.

When you get home, you wonder why, that you had even gone. You think, I'll have a cup of tea, and put the kettle on.

❉   ❉   ❉

Your friend phones you up, who makes you laugh, it's better than those pills. Cause if you believe what you do read that laughter cures all ills.

A Nudist Beach At Southwold?

A nudist beach at Southwold, or is this just a joke?
It would make the town quite seedy, and upset the local
folk.
On the beach it's got those little huts that sell for forty
grand, they don't want all those nudies cavorting in the
sand.

       ❈   ❈   ❈

It would scare off all the old folk they wouldn't know
where to look, cause you'd get some who were curious
and peep behind a book.
If they want to get their kit off couldn't they do it late
at night? So no one sees them skinny-dipping under the
pale moonlight.

       ❈   ❈   ❈

Who are these local councillors who want to push
this through? Intent to flaunt their naked flesh and
spoil the tasteful view.
Why don't they join a naturist club if nudity they seek?
To spoil that lovely Southwold beach they've got a bare
faced cheek.

With no pockets on their person where do they keep
their change? And where do they put their phones and
keys? That does seem rather strange.
It could lure some undesirables to Southwold's little
town, some politicians might be tempted including
Gordon Brown.

❋   ❋   ❋

They should have it down at Hollesley Bay
with the open prison next door, if the prisoners
saw that awful sight they wouldn't escape no
more.

Afternoon Tea

Christmas is coming the goose is getting fat, I must pop to Southwold, to buy a nice big hat. I like to look quite regal whilst shopping at my leisure, and buy a crate of sherry, to sip with utter pleasure.

❈   ❈   ❈

I made mince pies and sausage rolls, I had them ready at three. And put them on a doily, as the vicar's coming to tea.

❈   ❈   ❈

I switched on the gramophone, to add a touch of cheer. And then applied my lipstick, as he would soon be here.

❈   ❈   ❈

The vicar had four sherries, and then a glass of whisky. He was swaying to Perry Como, I hope he won't get frisky.

❈   ❈   ❈

We both were rather merry, and started dancing to the beat. The vicar nearly tripped me up, as he has two left feet.

❈   ❈   ❈

I got awfully worried, I really felt the heat. I said, *"Oh come on Reverend Shelley, have something else to eat."*

But Reverend Bob said, *"Oh no let's dance, you really do move well."* He was utterly sozzled, I could really tell.

❀   ❀   ❀

He said, *"Let's try a tango"* and grabbed me by the waist. To be in that position, wasn't really to my taste.

❀   ❀   ❀

I tried to give a little push, but he fell to the floor, I heard a car pull up outside, and my husband walked through the door.

❀   ❀   ❀

He just stood there speechless, the vicar struggled to his feet, my husband said, *"Good lord, what a way to meet!"*

❀   ❀   ❀

The red-faced vicar shook his hand and said, *"I must have had a fall, I'll see you at the carol service, merry Christmas to you all."*

All Work And Not Much Play

Some people work for many years in jobs that they detest. They work long hours for little pay, to give their kids the best.

❊ ❊ ❊

They want to increase the years you work, before you get your pension. But when you work in lousy jobs, it can cause a lot of tension.

❊ ❊ ❊

It's ok if you've an office job, or a job you love to do. But when you're doing manual work it takes it out of you.

❊ ❊ ❊

Working in a kitchen or serving up some food. Isn't very easy cause people are so rude.

The nurses in the hospitals, they work for little pay,
they'd get the same as politicians, if I had my way.

✿   ✿   ✿

It must be nice to go to work with colleagues that you
like, and when the boss steps out of line, tell him,
"Get on yer bike."

✿   ✿   ✿

And what if you are self-employed, with tax returns to
do, if you're late returning them, they slap a fine on
you.

✿   ✿   ✿

The best jobs they are on T.V. presenting or reading
News, the money they are earning, keeps them in
Jimmy Choos.

Barbara And The Bin Men

When Barbara saw the bin men, she began to shout,
"They haven't took me garbage, I never took it out."
She dashed out in a hurry, with her bin in tow.
I wonder if I'll catch them, afore they flippin go!

❊ ❊ ❊

She stood there in her curlers, out upon the
street, wearing just a nightie, and slippers
on her feet.

❊ ❊ ❊

Down the road she hurtled, with a pounding heart,
"You missed me, am I too late?" *"No! Jump up on the cart."*

❊ ❊ ❊

Her bin now isn't so heavy, cause she's gone kinda
green, no cardboard, mags, or bottles, nowhere to be
seen.

❊ ❊ ❊

She takes them down the bottle bank and with her
papers too, so if they miss her bin again, she'll know
just what to do.

Being Left Handed

Why is everything made right-handed it makes things
very fraught, the teacher when I was at school,
said, *"Just write as you were taught."*

* * *

They took the pen from my left hand and stuck it
in my right, but I could only scribble, I tried with all
my might.

* * *

My writing books were always smudged, cause I wrote
from left to right. And when my work went to be
marked it weren't a pretty sight.

* * *

The gadgets now are just as bad; the leads get in the
way. I wish that they would alter them, so they
go the other way.

If you hold the phone with your left hand and listen
with your left ear, it's hard to write a message, but
no one seems to care.
I had a mishap in the garden whilst using
secateurs, they tried to chop my finger off
that nearly caused some tears.

❊   ❊   ❊

It's just the same when ironing, I always do some harm,
when ironing shirts or linen I get iron marks
on my arm. And if you have to write a cheque, the
cheque books are all wrong, they open up the wrong
way round, so that takes twice as long.

❊   ❊   ❊

When seated at a table, or sitting on a plane,
try to sit on righty's left, cause it can be a pain.
You both start cutting up some food, your forks
they seem to clash, so just remember this advice,
when you're at another bash.

20

My son he is left handed, and my grandson too.
I suppose they got this curse off me, they seem to
muddle through. We've a lot in common with royal's,
Prince William's a lefty too, it hasn't stopped
him getting on, he's flying aircraft too.

❀   ❀   ❀

I think I'll form a lefty club, so we can swap advice.
Some brainchild might just save the day, and invent
some great device.

Blanche's Trip To Bluewater

Now Blanche she went to Bluewater to do some
Christmas shopping, she spotted Santa's grotto and
said, *"In here I'm popping."*
Santa said, *"You're kind of old my dear to get a Santa
treat,"* but Blanche she sidled up to him and said,
"I think you're neat."

❊   ❊   ❊

I love a man in red; with hairs all round his chin,
I think she was quite sozzled cause she'd been on the
gin, she said, *"I've especially come to see you, I've
waited for a year,"* but poor old Santa trembled, his face
was full of fear.
Blanche said, *"Oh don't be bashful"* her face was full of
glee, when Santa's elves came toddling in she was
sitting on his knee.

❊   ❊   ❊

She was a hefty lady, too heavy for him to bear, there
was a sound of creaking she broke poor Santa's chair.
She left the grotto rather sheepish and headed further
on; when suddenly she spotted her idol that tactile chap
Gok Wan.
She said *"Oh Mr Gok I love your show can I be a
volunteer?"* Gok said *"Oh well I'll have to see just go
stand over there."*

Well he took Blanche round the clothes shops to find
some saucy bits, he picked her out this low cut frock
that hardly covered her chest.
She said, *"Oh Mr. Gok I can't wear that, you know
I'm eighty four"*
Gok said, *"with your voluptuous figure they'll all be
wanting more."*

❀ ❀ ❀

So the camera started rolling, she began to strut her
stuff, she then got naked straight away and stood there
in the buff.
Gok clapped and cheered and wrapped a robe around
old Blanche's frame, she said, *"I've had a super time can I
come back again?"*

❀ ❀ ❀

She's waiting now to see herself on Gok's Show
on Channel Four, I think she'll wait a long long time
it's on the cutting room floor.

Cecil Lost One Wife Then Got A Life

Cecil was getting much too large he had this wobbly belly, and in his orange shell suit he looked just like a jelly.
He sat about and never worked, just eating crisps and drinking beer, he got by on all his benefits so he didn't really care.

        ✿   ✿   ✿

His wife she upped and left him for a toy boy tall and dark, she met him when he was working, as tree surgeon at the park.
She couldn't resist his six-pack, or the twinkle in his eye, she thought, I like the look of him, I'd like to date this guy.

        ✿   ✿   ✿

She goes off on his motorbike in sexy skintight leather, she knew this was the life she yearned, they went everywhere together.
Cause Cecil knew he had to change if he was to find another, he went off to his local gym with his mate and younger brother.
He cut out all the junk food and stopped watching daytime telly, the weight was quickly dropping off, and he lost his wobbly belly.

He came off all his benefits and works hard on the land, he's dating a well-known singer with a country and western band.
Cecil is now a different man he works to pay his way, he now enjoys a social life and won't have it any other way.

Dame Vera Lynn

Now who would have thought that Vera Lynn
would now be in the charts, this lady sang with
great band names and of course was the Force's
sweetheart.
She sang with Joe Loss and Charlie Kunz and
then the Bert Ambrose band, the serving troupes all
loved her, her voice echoed round the land.

❊   ❊   ❊

She sent messages to those brave lads, and visited
hospitals all over, with her famous song We'll Meet
Again and Blue Birds Over The White Cliffs of Dover.
She had her own radio show, it was called Sincerely
Yours, she met the soldiers' families whilst she was on
her tours.

❊   ❊   ❊

But she never became a diva she could teach those
girls now a thing or two, she was always very down
to earth, a lady through and through.
I know my era was the sixties, but I loved a good old
song, my mum played them on the wireless and we all
sang along.

26

You could hear what they were singing then the diction
was quite clear, most young girls now just shout and
wail, the melody's gone I fear.
You can tell now if a song is good if you can hum it
when you've heard it played but how many songs
can you hum to now? Just one or two I'd say.

Dante's Veggie Diet

Now Dante is a Norfolk cat, he really is unique,
his coat is truly sumptuous he has a great
physique.
He was deserted as a kitten and found in some
back street, but his new owner rescued him and
tried to make him eat.

❋   ❋   ❋

She cooked him tasty chicken but he
weren't having that, he then refused a plate
of fish he's such a complex cat.
He loves Brussels sprouts and carrots, without
a hint of meat, and rhubarb and asparagus, just
for a little treat.

❋   ❋   ❋

The veg he has is all homegrown tinned cat
food he won't touch he also nicks bananas he
likes them very much.
So Dante's vegetarian he don't like the look of
mice, nor chases birds and killing them because
he's just too nice.

❋   ❋   ❋

He's black, with white all on his chest and feet
like four white pads, he should be on telly
especially in them ads.

Doreen's Mobility Scooter

Doreen was getting rather frail, she couldn't walk
that far, she used to have a bicycle and never drove a
car.
She was a jovial lady who liked to have some fun,
she'd seen those nippy scooters, and said, *"I must get
one, they can't be very hard to drive, I think I'll be ok,
I'll take one for a test drive, and pop down there today."*

❀   ❀   ❀

There were several types to pick from, some small and
some quite large; she fancied one in purple that was
easier for her to charge.
The salesman was very helpful he gave her good advice
*"Be careful you don't hit someone, that wouldn't be
very nice."*

❀   ❀   ❀

She said, *"I'll need a trailer, a horn and lights that flash,
it will be very useful when to the shops I dash."*
The salesman said, *"We'll fit them all, it's going to look
unique, you'll soon be off to Lidl to get your shopping for the
week."*

She parked in a disability space, but the time she'd over
looked, then loaded up the trailer and saw that she'd
been booked.
By then a crowd had gathered round, to inspect her
strange machine, to get a parking ticket that was
bloomin' mean.

❅   ❅   ❅

She got back in her carriage and switched on her
flashing light, her two-tone horn began to sound
it played a carol Silent Night. She saw Santa standing
quite nearby but he was looking sad, he said, *"I've got
no transport I do feel very bad."*

❅   ❅   ❅

So Doreen said, *"Oh never fear my trailer is at hand"*
so Santa sat in the back of it, he did look rather grand.
She drove him round to all the shops where he had to
do his duty; he said, *"I really love your carriage it really
is a beauty."* So Doreen and her scooter went out on
several nights, she took Santa in her trailer to switch on
the Christmas lights.

Elf And Safety In The Fire Service

My husband was a fireman for twenty-five years or
more, when he read the daily paper he was shocked at
what he saw.

* * *

When they need to check the smoke alarms they
mustn't stand on those small steps, it's getting quite
ridiculous says the union reps. They climb up higher
ladders to rescue cats from trees, and crawl through
smoke filled tunnels whilst on their hands and knees.

* * *

They used to carry people over their shoulders, to
rescue them from fire, those ladders they were fifty
foot, they couldn't get much higher.
They don't give them now, a fireman's lift, it's all
hydraulic gear, them rules and regulations,
they change them every year.

When they're cooking food at lunchtime unless they get
a shout, they mustn't leave it in the oven they have to
take it out.
Or they could set off the smoke alarms and they're high
up on the wall, cause they mustn't stand on bloomin
steps in case they have a fall.

❋   ❋   ❋

Will they let them go to fires? Or will they get too hot?
So will elf and safety intervene and say they've got to
stop.
So you fireman just be careful, when you want to
change a socket, just have a copy of these rules,
stuffed in your shirt pocket.

Elsie

Elsie was lonely she wanted a life, she had twenty-eight
years of being a wife.
He'd gone off with a Philippino he met her on line,
and now he was having a whale of a time.
The girl couldn't have been fussy, he didn't look that
great, but she wanted to meet him and go on a date.
He said he was single and lived all alone, of course she
was smitten she needed a home.

✤   ✤   ✤

He shew her the house when Elsie went out, she was
looking in cupboards and pulling things out.
"Those clothes were my mothers" he lied through his
teeth, *"Oh she was a large lady, enormous, good grief."*
He knew his wife Elsie would soon be right back,
but she came home and caught them saw her clothes in
a sack.

✤   ✤   ✤

The Philippino and him were kicked out the door
"Don't you come back don't want you no more."
So Elsie was ready to go out and club, she found a nice
toy boy she met in a pub, he loved her full curves, and
her womanly look, he said, *"you're just like that pin up
I've seen in this book."*

I like something to cuddle, not bones that dig in,
don't like little beanpoles who look much too thin.
So Elsie and toy boy are living the life,
and Elsie once more will be somebody's wife.

Henry's Dating Game

Old Henry lived alone now, his kids didn't visit that
much, and all his other relatives, well they just all lost
touch.
He was getting rather lonely with no lady in his life,
but he didn't want a replacement for his beloved wife.
He wanted a lady for days out, and to have some
leisure, but he didn't want one of those hussies
that offered men some pleasure.

❀   ❀   ❀

He joined a dating agency and paid a hefty fee,
they called him up the very next day and said,
"We've found you three."
The first ones fifty four, with long blond curly hair,
the second was a red head, the third was mousy fair.
Now Henry was quite eager to meet these damsels
three, he said, *"I wonder if I'll like them or if they fancy
me."*

❀   ❀   ❀

The agency sent their photos and the hobbies they
partake, but when he met the red head it was a big
mistake.
Her only hobby was knitting and sitting in a chair,
so he quickly crossed her off the list and said, "I'll get
the next one here."
The next one was a mousy blond and all she did was
rabbit, she colour coded all Henry's clothes but he
couldn't stick that habit.

Then came Fifi with long blond hair, she was stacked like Diana Dors, she was very tactile and saw to all the chores.
Now Henry couldn't resist her, he fell for all her charms, but when he saw her get undressed she had hair all up her arms.
Cos Henry's sight weren't very good, and of course he didn't twig, when he started getting amorous on the pillow he spied her wig.

❈   ❈   ❈

Then Fifi said, *"You've rumbled me my real name is Joe but I feel like a woman, I thought you wouldn't know."*
So Henry lives alone again, but he's joined lots of clubs, he meets up with the friends he's made and pops down all the pubs.

Ladies In Makeup

I was looking at the makeup in Boots the other day,
when two smart ladies quite nearby started to walk my
way.
This makeup's so expensive the older woman said,
 "If I paid all that money it would just upset my Fred."

❃ ❃ ❃

There were several offers on, when you buy two get
one free, but we don't need to buy in bulk just cheaper
would suit me.
I said, *"With all these offers you don't save any money,
you forget where you have put them and that isn't very funny."*

❃ ❃ ❃

Those lipsticks I have bought before I don't know
where they are, they're not inside my cupboard they
must be melted in the car.
One lady picked up some foundation in a tiny little pot,
she said, *"This nearly nineteen quid much more than I
have got."*

She said, *"My face aint worth all that there's just too many cracks, I'll just stick to Nivea and buy some cheap mud packs."*
Some mascara make lashes longer, and make your eyes look wider, but if you put it on too thick they just look like a spider.

※　　　※　　　※

I said, *"Why don't you book a makeover they show you how to apply it."*
Oh yes she said, a good idea I really think I'll try it.
The make up girl had over heard she said, *"I've got a space, just come and sit down over here I'll soon sort out your face."*

※　　　※　　　※

She cleansed and toned the lady's face and then applied some gel, then picked up some foundation and slapped that on as well.
She then put on red lipstick and mascara on her eyes, *"You know when I have finished you'll have a big surprise."* By now the lady has had enough and feeling rather weary,
her husband Fred who then walked in said, *"Wow! I thought you were Julian Clary."*

Little Archie's Card

Little Archie was finding it jolly hard to make his mum
a Mother's Day card, he wanted to make one for a
surprise so he had to hide from prying eyes. He
searched for ribbons and bits of stuff, he had to be sure
he had quite enough.
He found buttons and card and a pot of glue,
Oh! He thought, I think this will do. He sat in his
bedroom and started to draw, then stuck on some bits
but then needed more.

❊   ❊   ❊

He cut off some buttons from dad's old shirt; he
thought dad wouldn't notice, so that won't hurt.
He needed some fabric, he had to think, he went in
mum's drawer and grabbed something pink. He cut out
some card and made lots of stickers, then cut out a
chunk from mum's pink knickers. It was nearly
finished and looking quite grand, he finished it off with
a little pink band.

❊   ❊   ❊

But later that evening, when they were off out, he
heard noises upstairs, mum started to shout. There's a
great big hole, in these knickers I bought, they cost me
five quid, they weren't seconds, I thought. Then mum
looked at dad, with sheer utter horror, your shirt
buttons have gone, thus going back tomorrow!

But on Mothers Day morning, she had a surprise, she saw Archie's card, and tears filled her eyes. It was quite an achievement, from her small wee boy, his face said it all, a picture of joy.

M & S Penny Bazaar

Marks and Spencer thought they'd go back in
time when everything cost a penny,
so all those people queued for hours I've never
seen so many.
They stood in line with bags in hand hoping to
get bargain stuff, one lady said, *"Now don't you push
there's sure to be enough."*

❀   ❀   ❀

When they opened up the doors there was a
great stampede, the assistant said, *"Just five
things each we can't have all this greed."*
This bloke grabbed all these knickers and took
them to the till, he said, *"They're for my girlfriend
they'll give her such a thrill."*

❀   ❀   ❀

He said, *"I don't know what size she is but I don't
suppose she'll care, she likes them in this leopard print they'll
last her all the year."*
A woman picked up some slippers, she had
three pairs in black, the assistant said *"just five
things each you'll have to put one back."*
But then I'll have an odd one; I'll have two pairs
and one spare, the assistant snatched one
slipper back she didn't seem to care.

41

This bloke took a suit to the till, he picked one out of many, the girl said, *"Oh you can't have that, thus not going for a penny."*
He said, *"I thought that it included everything, a penny for the day,"* the poor girl looked embarrassed she didn't know what to say.
He said, *"I'll speak to Twiggy cause she'll be on my side, I've queued up here for several hours I've been taken for a ride."*

❋   ❋   ❋

These other ladies then joined in, they were kicking up a stink they'd been queuing up all morning and got one can of drink.
"Oh we've had enough of this, there's no more penny stock, we'll pop to Stacey's from Eastenders market stall and buy a sexy frock."

My Friend's Trip To Felixstowe

My friend Dotty came to Felixstowe and went to
M and S, she wanted some new underwear and a
woolly winter dress.
She is a rotund lady, the curves she have are plenty,
the assistant said, *"Those drawers won't fit you'll need a
large size twenty."*

❊   ❊   ❊

But Dotty got all touchy she said, *"I'm just size ten, so
you take all them big things back I'll try these smaller
ones again."*
She picked up all these skimpy clothes and went to try
them on, *"I don't want these apple gatherers I'd like a
sexy thong".*

❊   ❊   ❊

The assistant heard strange noises coming from behind
the curtain, she called out, *"Do you think they'll fit?*
Dotty said, *"Yes I'm certain,"*
The assistant heard an awful noise that sounded like a
rip, but Dotty said, *"Oh do clear off you're getting on my
pip."*

Of course the clothes didn't fit at all, the dress clung like a vice, the visible panty line was all too clear and didn't look very nice.

She said, *"I'm not shopping here no more"* the assistant said, *"Good heavens, why don't you pop to Ipswich and find that shop called Evans."*

❊   ❊   ❊

Well Dotty finally got her clothes she looked like Joe Brand's double, I'm not going shopping with her no more, she's too much bloomin trouble.

My Lost Mail

That postal strike was such a pain my letters all went
astray, the birthday cards I sent last week haven't got
there to this day.
I sealed them down with first class stamps and dropped
them in the mail, made sure they didn't weigh too
much, all this to no avail.

❀   ❀   ❀

I was going to buy a scooter and deliver them by hand,
and have a satnav fitted, so I don't get lost you
understand.
I could whiz around with my Christmas cards they'd
get there mighty quick, save money on the postage and
have no stamps to lick.

❀   ❀   ❀

I'd be known as Jane the postie when you see me
on my route, and if people take the mickey I couldn't
give a hoot.
Of course I can't deliver parcels my scooter wouldn't
take all that weight, I'll send them with Eddie Stobart
and they can go as freight.

❀   ❀   ❀

I'm sorry if my cards didn't come, don't think that
I forgot, cause sending birthday greetings it really
means a lot.

Now I've Got Me Bus Pass

Now I've got me bus pass, I thought I'd use the bus, all loaded down with shopping, what a flipping fuss.

❀   ❀   ❀

Have them seats got smaller, or have I just got wide, I can't shift up no more, I'm near the edge I cried.

❀   ❀   ❀

A lady squeezed beside me, shoved her shopping on me lap, I couldn't get off at my next stop, so I was in a flap.

❀   ❀   ❀

I called out, *"Hey you missed me stop, what am I supposed to do?"* The driver said, *"Well that's your tough luck, didn't ring the bell, you silly moo."*

❀   ❀   ❀

I'll really have to use the car, when I've got heavy shopping, 'cos after carrying all them bags, I'm just fit for dropping.

❀   ❀   ❀

I'll use it less for smaller trips, now petrol's gone sky high, and what about that flipping bus, I'll give it one more try.

46

On The Cutting Room Floor

Maureen had long auburn hair, it came right down her
back, she didn't look over fifty, her face didn't have
one crack.

❁   ❁   ❁

She was going somewhere special and thought she'd
have a trim, so she phoned up Trevor's Salon, and they
quickly booked her in.

❁   ❁   ❁

She went off to the salon, sat in the swivel chair,
Trevor said, *"It's got quite long, how much do you want off
here?"*

❁   ❁   ❁

Oh she said, just a little bit, my husband likes long hair,
and if I had it snipped too short, it could give him
quite a scare.

❁   ❁   ❁

But Trevor lost concentration, he started talking to
Mrs. Peat, he rushed back and started cutting, he
said, *"You'll soon be looking neat."*

❁   ❁   ❁

He must have had a memory lapse, he was chopping it
off quite quick, he said, *"My scissors will need sharpening,
your hair is jolly thick."*

Now Maureen trusted Trevor, she'd been going there
for years, but she dozed off for a little while, when she
woke she was in tears.

❊   ❊   ❊

He'd cut it short, right to the nape, her locks lay on the
floor, she howled in disbelief, couldn't believe the sight
she saw.

❊   ❊   ❊

Oh Trevor I only said a trim, what have you gone and
done? It's shorter than Anne Robinson's, I really
shouldn't have come.

❊   ❊   ❊

Poor Trevor knew it was too late, he couldn't glue it
back, if he couldn't calm down Maureen, he knew he'd
get the sack.

❊   ❊   ❊

He said, *"Oh Maureen you look younger now, it's taken years
off you, your husband will think it's sexy, you'll get to love it
too."*

You can be my model; you'll get your hair done free for life, your husband will save his money, with less to pay his wife.

❀ ❀ ❀

Cause Maureen now had changed her mind, she couldn't give a fig, cause if she wanted it long again, she could always wear a wig.

Our Dog Jason

We had a wirehaired Fox Terrier he was a funny little
boy, the tricks that he got up to, he brought us years of
joy.

❊　　❊　　❊

He would never sit or stay or do as he was told, he had
selective hearing he was always very bold.

❊　　❊　　❊

He loved a cup of tea and ate anything in sight,
and if he saw a piece of cake he would always take a
bite.

❊　　❊　　❊

One night when taking him out for walks I just began
to squirm, cause sticking out of his other end
looked like a great big worm.

❊　　❊　　❊

I stood on it but it went ping Jason gave a great big
yell, he shot halfway down the road Just like a bat
from hell.

When I caught poor Jason the worm was three foot
long, I was getting very worried there's something very
wrong.

❀ ❀ ❀

I phoned my husband at the fire station to tell him what
was wrong, he got home in minutes it didn't take him
very long.

❀ ❀ ❀

By now poor Jason's very stressed we took him to the
vet, we had to get it sorted he was a much-loved pet.

❀ ❀ ❀

The vet pulled yards and yards out of his rear
he said *"It isn't plastic, your Jason's eaten a golf ball
with yards and yards of elastic."*

The vet had to do what he had to do while Jason stood on the table, however did he eat that ball? However was he able?

✿   ✿   ✿

I was just so glad it weren't a worm it made me feel quite bad and when my husband got the bill it made him feel quite sad.

✿   ✿   ✿

Those firemen on my husband's watch wouldn't let it go away, they said is Jason under par or is he going out today?

✿   ✿   ✿

They said, *"What is his handicap?"* I really took some stick, he's waiting for his walkies I better tee off quick.

52

People's Pets

Some people like to have a pet to keep them company
in their home, they bring lots of pleasure when people
live alone.
It may be a little dog who likes to have a walk, they can
tell you lots of things even though they cannot talk.
They're always pleased to see you when you come
through the door, and when you cook them something
tasty they always look for more.

     ❊   ❊   ❊

When I had my dog some years ago he brought us lots
of joy, he was a little character a funny little boy.
He always loved a cup of tea and slurped it straight
away, of course he liked a biscuit too he had this every
day.

     ❊   ❊   ❊

I thought I'd lost him one day, he was nowhere to be
seen, I searched the house and then outside and
retraced where I had been. I'd been and hung the
washing out, and popped to see old Ted, and then I
went to get the pegs out of the garden shed.
So I went back down the garden and opened the old
shed door, and there was Jason sitting there quite
happy on the floor.

Syd-E-Ney The Head Waiter

My friend Syd-E-Ney was a waiter at a posh hotel,
he had us all in stitches with yarns he had to tell.
There was this classy lady, who at the table had a nap
she woke up quick and knocked her plate, her soup
went in her lap.

❃   ❃   ❃

She wailed! *"Oh dear what can I do? my skirt it's soaked
right through."*
Syd-e-ney said, *"I'll look inside lost property and see what I
can do."*
But the lady she was tiny, a skirt had to be quite small,
he could only find a large mans kilt, and this was an
evening ball.

❃   ❃   ❃

She said, *"Oh I'm not Scottish that kilt it just won't do"*
Syd said, *"Just wear it for a little while 'cos yours is soaked
right through."*
He helped her wrap the skirt around, and fastened it
with a pin, she said, *"Oh this smells funny, I don't know
where it's bin."*

❃   ❃   ❃

The kilt came down to her ankles, you could only see
her feet, Syd said, *"I'll fetch you something special so you
can have a treat."*
He came back with the best champagne and she just
knocked it back, I better keep her sweet he thought or
I might get the sack.

Well the lady got so merry, and she began to sing,
she lifted her kilt up off the floor, and done a highland
fling.
'Cos then headwaiter Syd-E-Ney had nearly done his
shift he had a call from the penthouse suite, to take
breakfast up in the lift.

❀　　❀　　❀

He got in the lift quite smartish, full English on a tray
but when the lift stopped, there was a jolt,
two fried eggs and a sausage got away.
The lift went down without him, he thought I'll have to
get some more, but when he finally caught the lift,
eggs and sausage were on the floor.

❀　　❀　　❀

But no one saw this happen, young Syd-E-Ney acted
quick, he flipped eggs and sausage on the plate,
and reached the penthouse in a tick.
The colonel who was still in bed, well he just woofed it
down, he patted Syd-E-Ney on the back and gave him
half a crown.

❀　　❀　　❀

That breakfast was amazing, those eggs were quite
sublime, *"Can you bring me two more the same if you can find
the time?"*

The Antiques Road Show

I went to Somerleyton Thursday to see the Antiques
Road Show, the queues were long and winding and
moving very slow.
I never took my valuables in case they all got nicked,
but I watched all the goings on to see who the experts
picked.

❊   ❊   ❊

Some people took a load of tat, I've seen better in a
skip, but we enjoyed the sunny day it was a pleasant
trip.
Now Hilary Kay was at her table valuing this and that,
when this old boy came over, they had a good old chat.
He had these speckled birds with him, found off
Blakeney on a wreck, she said, *"I like the look of these"*
He said *"Oh bloomin heck."*

❊   ❊   ❊

He said, *"You're prettier in the flesh"* and then he
called her darling, she asked, *"What is your name sir?"*
He said, *"My name is Starling."*
She had tears of laughter down her face, she said,
*"I want you on the show, I don't know much
about your birds but someone else might know."*
Some people took their jewellery, post-cards and some
Books, this lady took this great big pig she got some
funny looks.

56

The Apple Gatherers

When Joseph picked the apples from off his apple tree,
he thought oh yummy yummy, apple pie for tea.

❖   ❖   ❖

He took them into Barbara for her to peel and core,
and left another bag full outside the kitchen door.

❖   ❖   ❖

She said, *"I don't make apple pies you know, I'll put on
too much weight. Just bag 'em up and price 'em, and leave 'em
by the gate."*

❖   ❖   ❖

When they went out for the day, and came home rather
late.
They saw the apples all had gone, and thought, oh this
is great.

❖   ❖   ❖

She counted out the money, it didn't seem to add, she
spied a piece of paper, she said, *"I have been had."*

❖   ❖   ❖

An unknown person took them, and left an I.O.U.
It said, *"I'll pop back later and pay you what is due."*

The weeks went by, and still no sign of scrumpers, or
their money, to nick two bags of apples really isn't
funny.

❈   ❈   ❈

It was going to charity, but now they will be short,
the apple nicking tea leaf is still being sought.

The Cow Boy Plumber

My friend wanted a brand new bathroom she had to
find a man to plumb, she phoned a man in yellow pages
and said, *"When can you come?"* He said,
"I'll come as soon as poss." a job he had to do, so he came
round the very next day, and said *"What can I do for
you?"*

❋   ❋   ❋

She shew him a little picture, she'd cut out from a book,
he said, *"I'll get my measure and go and have a look."* She
wanted a freestanding bathtub with gold taps and all
the frills, and tiles all round, and on the floor in case of
any spills.

❋   ❋   ❋

He took six days to fit it, he wasn't in a rush, she
couldn't wait to try it out and go and have a flush.
He'd put the shower in position but it wasn't good at
all, he'd only put it three feet high, and she was six foot
tall.

"How can I take a shower with that? It only comes up to my thigh, he said, *"Well just sit in the bath and use it, you don't need it very high.* It says you've got the Corgi stamp when I read it in yellow pages, *"Oh I told a little porky that training it takes ages."*

✽   ✽   ✽

She pulled the chain on the toilet so she could see it flush, but the water shot out of the showerhead it came out with a gush. She turned the taps on that were fixed to the bath they came off in her hand, he said, *"That never usually happens I just don't understand."*

✽   ✽   ✽

He said, *"I need a cup of tea 'cos I am feeling bad, I should have gone to college and listened to my Dad."*
"Oh I've had enough of you, go and don't come back, I'm not paying you any money, I'm giving you the sack."

The Credit Crunch

My friend's husband Jim has lost his job because
of the credit crunch, he hardly dared to tell her, he
couldn't eat his lunch.
He'd worked hard as a pastry chef for many
many years, he never dreamed that his hard
work would only end in tears.

❊   ❊   ❊

He used to have an ice cream van, he was
known as Mr. Jingle, he got up to many tricks
when he was young and single.
The girls all loved his ninety nines he gave them
an extra dollop, but one called Maeve kept
stalking him she was a bloomin' trollop.

❊   ❊   ❊

He'd drive along at such a speed his cornets
all got crushed, when he saw Maeve awaiting he
got hot and flushed.
This other bird called Susan he began to date
she used to phone him all the time she said,
"Don't you be late."

She used to cycle everywhere, where he would
park his van, she said, *"I'll do your soft scoops
'cos you just know I can."*
She used to hide her bicycle so neighbours
wouldn't know, they just saw the ice-cream van
swaying to and fro.

❊   ❊   ❊

She sat in the back of Jingles van eating all the
flakes, munching all the profits that poor old
Jimmy makes.
She didn't take long to dump him when
Giovanni nicked his pitch, she fell for his Italian
charms and 'cos he was quite rich.

❊   ❊   ❊

Now Jimmy soon recovered and married my
friend Wendy, now she's the apple of his eye
and very smart and trendy.
Tomorrow he's got an interview, for an M&S bra
fitter, of cos I just made that bit up, I thought it
would raise a titter!

The Deliverymen

My friend she bought a brand new fridge her other was
past it's prime, the shop said they'd deliver but couldn't
say what time.
She thought I'll empty the fridge when I get home,
there's lots of food still in it but if it's past the use by
date I'll just have to bin it.

* * *

She got back home at half past two, the new fridge
had been sent, her husband said, *"They took the fridge
and off with it they went."*
She said, *"Oh you must have emptied it, so where
did you put the grub?"*
He said, *"I left them to it and went down to the pub."*

* * *

There was steak in there and cottage pie and
bangers, and a curry, her husband said, *"I thought they
nipped off smartish as if they were in a hurry."*
She said *"I'm going to the depot to see what they have
done,"* the boss he said *"They're out the back in the staff
room having fun."*

She opened the door of the staff room there was a lovely smell of dinner, this bloke says, *"When we took that fridge we knew we were on a winner."*
He said, *" 'Cos it's my birthday and we thought we'd have a bash, just help yourself to cottage pie or bangers and some mash."*

❈   ❈   ❈

There's lager too they left in the fridge so we've just had a few, she never had the heart to tell them she thought she'd join in too.
They told her about a job last week when they picked up this freezer, 'cos when they opened up the lid out popped this naked geezer.

❈   ❈   ❈

He'd been seeing someone else's wife, and they were both in bed, her husband came home early and if he found him he'd be dead.
The wife said, *"Oh hurry up and hide here come my husband Jake,"* 'cos she'd forgot about the freezer some men were coming to take.

❈   ❈   ❈

They said, *"We do enjoy our work we don't know what we'll find, them people leaving all that grub they really are so kind."*

The Good Old Days

I read in the paper the other day, take an aspirin to
protect your heart, now it says don't take them
good lord where do we start?
We mustn't drink that full cream milk, and now not
even semi, but if all we can have is completely skimmed
I'd rather not have any.

❀   ❀   ❀

We never had this when I was young and people were
all thinner, with good old British meat and veg and lots
of spuds for dinner.
Most people eat in the evenings now instead of midday
dinner, perhaps there is a clue in that? Is that why they
were thinner?

❀   ❀   ❀

There's too much choice of crisps and snacks that are
eaten in between, we never had those years ago in the
shops they just weren't seen.
There weren't those supermarkets then, just the little
corner shop, if you ran out of milk or bread that's
where you had to pop.

Now Saturdays were quite a treat, with Dixon Of
Dock Green and Billy Cotton, we had a penny bags of
broken crisps, those days won't be forgotten.
We collected bottles down off the Denes by Lowestoft's
north end beach, we earned our pocket money then,
you got money back off each.

    ❊   ❊   ❊

No mobile phones and all that text, kids spoke in
English then, all this texting language sends folk round
the bend.
I wish they'd bring back old English speech with words
like whence, yonder, and loquacious,
the way they are speaking nowadays is simply quite
audacious.

The Heat Wave

I used to love hot sunny days when I was young and
bolder, but I can't wear bikini's now, that I am plump
and older.

❊   ❊   ❊

They used to call me Olive Oil, cos I was really thin,
so now I cover up some more, it really is a sin.

❊   ❊   ❊

I lay awake so hot to sleep, the covers on the floor,
shall I make a cup of tea? It's only ten to four.

❊   ❊   ❊

The fan is humming in my ears it makes a flipping row,
to lay and hear that blinking thing, I think I'll get up
now.

❊   ❊   ❊

I looked out of the window, the sky was really grey,
I think we're going to have some rain, bring it on I say.

❊   ❊   ❊

I really shouldn't moan so much, but there is work to
do. It's far too hot to Hoover, or get the iron out too.

I don't think I'll bother to get dressed, I'll Hoover in the buff, no one can see me, so who cares, and if they can! That's tough.

❀   ❀   ❀

I hope my husband don't pop home, or he might be perplexed, to see me looking starkers, he might get over sexed.

The Ice Cream Jingles

We're losing all the ice-cream vans, they just can't
make them pay, so the kids can't have a cornet when
they're out to play. We used to have one round near by,
kids listened for the jingle, the women got a great big
cone especially if they were single.

※　　※　　※

There was Tony Bells and Peters, and of course
Lorenzo's too, the children loved a ninety-nine,
whatever will they do?
We'll miss the sounds of Greensleeves echoing all
around, and children yelling ice cream man, and asking
for a pound.

※　　※　　※

They taste better off the ice cream man especially with
a flake, so we hope that they don't disappear I hope
they stay for goodness sake. My Dad he liked a wafer,
it looked just like a brick, they pressed the ice cream all
around, it was really nice and thick.

My little dog liked ice cream, he stole one off this man,
he'd just bent down to pat him when he stole his cone
and ran.
The man he couldn't stop laughing, he said no need to
worry, I caught my dog quite smartish and took him
home in quite a hurry.

※　　　※　　　※

All this talk of ice cream, I fancy one quite quick,
oh, I can hear a jingle I'll get one in a tick.

The New Shed

Our new shed arrived last week at last, it's firmly in its
place, the old one's gone for firewood, it looked a right
disgrace.
The new one's done with Cuprinol in a fetching spruce
green shade, I bought some nice net curtains, they
came already made.
They've got some yellow geese on them, a proper
farmyard scene, but they look like Norwich colours,
with the shed, that shade, of green.

❉   ❉   ❉

This shed I want kept tidy, with just some garden gear,
I don't want any muddy boots, or rubbish dumped in
there.
I'd like an armchair in it and a carpet on the floor,
I think I'll get a Keep Out sign and nail it on the door.
In the summer I'll write my poems in there but it's just
too cold as yet, a heater is really needed I haven't got
one yet.

I'll get a two-way radio, so my husband can keep in
touch, 'cos if I stay in there too long, he won't like it
very much.
Now he's got the garage, for all his tools and stuff,
the space he has is adequate, I think he's got enough.
'Cos my sherry takes up lots of space, it's a good
place for it to be, I'll ask the neighbours round quite
soon to have a drop with me.

The Police Flower Show

Reg and Maisie, grew all their own veg, swapped
cuttings with neighbours over the hedge.
They grew flowers and herbs and prize-winning
shrubs, won dozens of trophies with their plants in
large tubs.

❉   ❉   ❉

They took some of their herbs to the Police Flower
Show, there were several new plants their names I
don't know. Maisie made some infusions inside the
marquee, she brewed up some herbs and made some
green tea.

❉   ❉   ❉

The police chief inspector came in for a taste,
he drank several cups, didn't want any waste.
His lady wife Doris drank several cups too,
and the sergeant and his wife had drunk one or two.

❉   ❉   ❉

But a few moments later they were larking about
Inspector Blake and Doris were starting to shout.
They were jumping on chairs and getting quite frisky,
the judges all thought that they'd been on the whisky.

Their clothes were being scattered all over the ground,
the official in charge just had to be found.
Samples were taken of all the green tea and some other
strange plants the official could see.

        ❊   ❊   ❊

More herbs were taken they examined a lot,
but the plant Maisie brewed turned out to be pot.
Reg said, *"Oh Maisie what have you done now?"*
She said, *"Someone's been tampering but I just don't
know how."*

        ❊   ❊   ❊

This was an embarrassing episode, for the boys from
the nick, they wanted the whole thing hushed up, and
pretty damn quick.
Maisie was let off with a warning, from the top man in
blue, he said, *"Be careful in future of concoctions you
brew."*

The Sales

The sales are on it's time to shop the clothes are cheap
as chips, there's skirts and trousers to be had if you can
get them over your hips.
There's people pushing and shoving, trying to grab
what you have got, one lady snatched a shoe off me I
think she'd lost the plot.

❊　　❊　　❊

She said, *"I need these shoes I really do, cause they will
fit my mother."*
I said, *"Well unless she has only got one leg you'd better
take the other."*
She marched into the fitting room with a dress about
size eight, the assistant said, *"Excuse me mam, you'll
need a twenty-eight."*

❊　　❊　　❊

I read in the paper the other day your face ages
when you diet, so they can keep that slimming plan
'cos I don't think I'll try it.
All those people walking past they look young from
behind, but when you see the front of them,
their skins are like orange rind.

Those young girls who are models, their bones rattle when they walk, they ain't got no sexy curves, they're like a bloomin stalk.
Now Sophia Loren and Diana Dors, and Marilyn and Doris Day, they looked like real women, much nicer in every way.

❦   ❦   ❦

They led the way in fashion, and had a lot of style, and with all that talent, they went the extra mile.
So Chanel should do a U turn, and pick real women instead, to model on the catwalks, they would be streets ahead.

The Swinging Sixties

When I was a teenager in the sixties and out with my
friend Wendy, we used to go out quite a bit, we
thought we were dead trendy.
'Cos we were mods in those days, we liked the Vespas
with all those lights; we drank coffee in this little café to
pass away the nights.

❀   ❀   ❀

There were no skinny lattes or cappuccinos for you to
pick, there was just one type in Pyrex cups, all milky
and rather thick.
There was a jukebox there of course, it played three
records for a shilling, to hear great music all night long
was really rather thrilling.

❀   ❀   ❀

There was this rocker café across the road, big
bikes and all that leather, we were often tempted over
there but us mods, we stuck together.

We played this song by Twinkle called "Terry," but
very sad, he drove his bike quite recklessly the ending
was quite bad.
They banned it on the BBC in nineteen sixty-four, but
when they banned those songs on air you played them
even more.

❧ ❧ ❧

They banned "Tell Laura I Love Her," that also had a
tragic ending, I suppose they banned them at the BBC
because of the message they were sending.
I know I must be showing my age but don't you go and
jest, the Stones, the Searchers, and Manfred Mann
the old ones are the best.

The Trainee Hairdresser

The salon was getting very full, appointments were
double booked, the new girl had forgot to check, and in
the book she hadn't looked.
This chap was getting angry he'd been waiting
for a while, the trainee girl named Trixie said,
"I'll cut it." With a smile.

❖　　❖　　❖

He said, *"I've got a meeting so could you make it
quick?"* she said, *"I'll find some scissors I'll be back in a
tick."* She hadn't cut hair for clients before and so her
pulse was racing, she went into a cupboard and fetched
a pudding basin.

❖　　❖　　❖

She placed it on the client's head and snipped his
hair all round, but when she took the basin off you
couldn't hear a bloomin sound.
The man said, *"O gawd what have you done to me?
I've got a meeting at ten, you haven't had much
practice I look like the flower pot men."*

The salon owner then arrived, her face it turned
bright red, *"Oh Trixie what have you gone and done? That
bloke's my husband Fred."*
Now just go mix some colour for Mrs. Kelly
over there, I've left it on that table the one that says
shade fair.

❊   ❊   ❊

So Trixie mixed the colour while she chatted to Mrs.
Kelly, she said, *"I've seen you somewhere else before
have you been on the telly?"*
She dabbed the colour on her hair and then she set the
timer, she said, *"Are you off to somewhere nice?"*
"I'm going to Dolly's Diner."

❊   ❊   ❊

Young Trixie was getting peckish she said, *"I'll soon be
back, I'm just popping to the greasy spoon to get a little
snack."* She just finished her last few chips then broke
out in a sweat, *"Oh my lord, the colour, I haven't rinsed her
yet."*
She flew back to the salon and rinsed Mrs. Kelly's hair,
it had gone a shade of orange it wasn't at all shade fair.

She said, *"Oh what have you done to me?"* dripping in
the sink, *"I don't look like a sexy blond more like Anne
off The Weakest Link."*
So Trixie now is unemployed and looking for a job, she
said she might pop down to Felixstowe to have a word
with Bob.

The Vanishing Rooster

My friend she bought some chickens, to lay her free-
range eggs, there were five that were a brownie tan and
a black one with three legs.
She fed them on mash and lots of corn, and tucked
them up at night, but one morning there was only five,
this gave her such a fright.
The black one had gone missing, there were no feathers
anywhere, and she couldn't understand it she knew a
fox hadn't been in there.

❖　❖　❖

She'd named the black one Jake the peg, it ran faster
than the rest, and the eggs she laid were bigger and
better than the rest.
I wonder if she wandered to find some pasture new
"Oh well," she said, *"there's no good moping there's
nothing I can do."*
The other five were fretting, they missed their
feathered friend, they weren't laying any eggs, this sent
her round the bend.

When she popped to Bungay for some sausages the other day, she passed the Ditchingham roundabout as it was on the way.

She saw the famous chickens that have always roosted there, and then suddenly from nowhere old Jake she did appear.

She was with another chicken who happened also to be black, they looked so very happy she couldn't take her back.

❊   ❊   ❊

Instead she bought two new ones, they've settled down quite well, the others soon perked up again I don't think they could tell.

The eggs were coming thick and fast with yolks as rich as gold, I popped round to buy some but of course they'd all been sold.

She often drives the Ditchingham way to see if Jakes ok, she's still strutting round large as life and is still there to this day.

❊   ❊   ❊

It's a mystery still how Jake escaped, I suppose we'll never know, the hen house now's been reinforced so her precious hens can't go.

She says, *"I hope the weather soon warms up, my chucks don't like cold feet, and if they can't get warm quite soon there'll be no eggs to eat."*

Time To Do The Garden

It's time to get some pansies to decorate my pots,
and tidy up the garden it's full of forget-me-nots.
I'll have to get my trowel and fork and have a dig
around, there's plenty of jolly weeds springing out of
the ground.

❈   ❈   ❈

We'll pop down to the nursery to look at all the
flowers, to get it looking shipshape takes my husband
lots of hours.
Last year I put some bulbs in, I found them in the shed
but I didn't get any daffodils I'd planted onion bulbs
instead.

❈   ❈   ❈

I grew some herbs in little pots, some basil, mint, and
dill, I must have chopped some weeds instead 'cos I
was really ill. I think I'll grow some carrots it may
improve my sight, so when I chop them herbs again I
may just get it right.

84

Welcome Prime Minister

When I was in Southwold the other day, dippin' me toes in the sea. Gordon lickin' an ice cream, came waddling up to me.

❋ ❋ ❋

"I live at No.10 you know, and I've come here for a treat, Sarah's gone to Lowestoft to get some fish to eat."

❋ ❋ ❋

"The kids are in the beach hut playing with some sand. The beach hut was a bargain, a snip at seventy grand."

❋ ❋ ❋

Why don't you go to Oulton Broad, and go on them power boats, that would look good in the papers, and might pull in some votes.

❋ ❋ ❋

Why not try jogging to Pleasurewood Hills, but don't go get a blister, there's a nice new ride that might suit you, I think it's called the twister.

❋ ❋ ❋

Or you could nip to Thorpeness, a rowing boat you could take, go out as far as you can row, and then jump in the lake.

When Dolly Gate Crashed

Aunt Dolly was sitting having a drink in a pub,
when she noticed some tables all stacked up with grub.
She thought, this is lovely what a nice treat I feel rather
peckish I've had nothing to eat.
There were quiches and vol-au-vents, and sarnies and
jelly, she soon got stuck in and filled up her belly.

※　　※　　※

But while she was eating her large piece of cake
she was suddenly aware she'd made a mistake.
Some people came in wearing suits and black tie,
she thought, they don't look happy, did somebody
die?
Dolly pretended to be a good family friend
and offered condolences to the chap on the end.

※　　※　　※

She said, *"I knew your poor Auntie your dear Auntie
Pam,"*
The man said, *"You what? It was her husband old Sam.
Pam's over there in that great big red hat, she lives all
alone now with her black and white cat."*

Dolly said, "*I live in that care home that's just up the road it's quite diabolical, and I don't like their food.*"
The matron weren't looking when she quietly sneaked out, she goes there quite often for a pint of milk stout.
There's an old boy who lives there who drinks too much whisky, he's after my body and gets rather frisky.
So Dolly's been rumbled, she gate-crashed their wake, she nipped out the back and her exit did make.

When Olga Became A Thespian

Now Olga was getting older, she hadn't had much fun,
she'd been quite prim and proper, and lived just like a
nun. She thought she'd like to live a bit, before she
pops her clogs, she liked old Terry Wogan,
and was one of his old togs.

❖   ❖   ❖

She thought she'd join a drama group, and perhaps
she'd act on stage, she fancied playing a racy part,
she thought she looked good for her age.
She went along to join the group, and to audition for a
part, they gave her just a walk on role, but that was just
a start.

❖   ❖   ❖

She enjoyed it there and made some friends, and
thought she'd found her niche, the producer was quite
handsome, in fact he was a dish.

She auditioned for a leading role as a sexy buxom wench, she'd have to be quite naked and sit on a wooden bench.
She read her lines, and strut her stuff and sat on a bench of wood, the producer thought, I'll dim the lights it might make her look half good.

❀   ❀   ❀

But halfway through the second act there was a mighty yell, Olga got a splinter in her rear and it really hurt like hell. The safety curtain soon came down so that tweezers could be found, the leading man, a carpenter extracted it safe and sound.

❀   ❀   ❀

Well Olga got her leading role she had a cushion for that seat, she really brought the house down and gave them all a treat.

While Barbara's Away

When Barbara went on holiday it was so very hot,
her poor old flowers and baskets thought they'd been
forgot.

✽   ✽   ✽

So off I went with a watering can to give them all a
drink. I watered pots, and welly boots, and even a
china sink.

✽   ✽   ✽

They're growing round the lily pond, and in the
flowerbed, pots and tubs in every space, right down to
the shed.

✽   ✽   ✽

It is a mass of colour, they're growing everywhere,
she'll plant her flowers in anything, she really doesn't
care.

✽   ✽   ✽

She knows where they're all hiding, she doesn't need
no stickers, I wouldn't be at all surprised, if they were
growing in her knickers.

East Anglia's Children's Hospices are delighted to benefit from sales of this book. Poetry holds a special place in our hearts as it often allows us the time to reflect for a few moments on life, whether it is funny or sad or a special moment.

Here at East Anglia's Children's Hospices, we try to make every day a special one. We help local life-threatened children and their families with the emotional and physical challenges they face by providing expert care and a range of other essential support in a home-from-home environment, or in the comfort of their own home.

I hope you will read and enjoy this book in the knowledge that it aims to support the children and families we care for at EACH.

Melanie Chew, Director of Fundraising
East Anglia's Children's Hospices

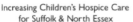

Increasing Children's Hospice Care
for Suffolk & North Essex